ANTARCTICA

by Catherine C. Finan

Minneapolis, Minnesota

Credits:

Title Page, 5 top left, 11 bottom left, Stu Shaw/Shutterstock; 4 top, Goinyk Production/Shutterstock; 4 bottom left, Taras Grebinets/Shutterstock; 5 top right, Vixit/Shutterstock; 5 bottom, Steve Heap/Shutterstock; 5 bottom left, Marko Poplasen/Shutterstock; 5 bottom right, Cast Of Thousands/Shutterstock; 6 top, Nevena Barberic/Shutterstock; 6 middle, Michael Lodge/Shutterstock; 6 bottom, Harvepino/Shutterstock; 7 upper top right, 17 top, NASA/Public Domain; 7 top, esOteric/Creative Commons; 7 top right, glenda/Shutterstock; 7 bottom, Mike Lucibella, NSF/Public Domain; 7 bottom left,Design Projects/Shutterstock; 7 bottom right, Louella938/Shutterstock; 4–5, 8, 20 top, 23 bottom, TESSIER Ewan/Creative Commons; 8 left, Andrey Arkusha/Shutterstock; 9 top, AmeliAU/Shutterstock; 9 middle, Foto 4440/Shutterstock; 9 bottom, Photodynamic/Shutterstock; 10 top, jeaneeem/Creative Commons; 10 top left, Joe Tabacca/Shutterstock; 10 top right, Taras Grebinets/Shutterstock; 10 middle, 11 middle, Photovolcanica.com/Shutterstock; 10 bottom, Edgeworth David/Public Domain;11 top, Alasdair Turner, GOLF 4-3-9 Antarctica Expedition 2012/Creative Commons; 11 bottom, Murray Foubiste·/Creative Commons; 11 bottom right, xolmgard/Shutterstock; 12 top, 12 bottom, Eli Duke/Creative Commons; 12 bottm left, Just dance/Shutterstock; 13 top, Daniel Prudek/Shutterstock; 13 middle, by_polyarnik/Shutterstock; 13 middle left, YaroslaVW/Shutterstock; 13 middle right, shipfactory/Shutterstock; 13 bottom top, Matthew Field/Creative Commons; 13 bottom, Red Tiger/Shutterstock; 14, National Science Foundation/Peter Rejcek/Public Domain; 14 bottom left, Herbert Ponting/Public Domain; 15 top, US Embassy New Zealand/Public Domain; 15 middle, 15 bottom, Jill Mikucki/University of Tennessee Knoxville/Creative Commons; 15 middle left, Juice Dash/Shutterstock;15 middle right, Pressmaster/Shutterstock; 16-17, 19 top, 25 middle, Christopher Michel/Creative Commons; 16 bottom, LightField Studios/Shutterstock; 17 middle, Fiona M. Donnelly/Shutterstock; 17 bottom, kallerna/Creative Commons; 17 bottom left, Anatoliy Karlyuk/Shutterstock; 18 Matt Cooper/Shutterstock; 18 bottom right, iofoto/Shutterstock; 19 bottom, United States Antarctic Program/Public Domain; 19 bottom left, Nick Starichenko/Shutterstock; 20 top left, Georg von Bothmann/Public Domain; 20 top right, Public Domain; 20 bottom, Temanu/Shutterstock; 21 top, Mbreen/Creative Commons; 21 middle, Antarctic Treaty Secretariat (ATS)/Creative Commons; 21 bottom, Hugh Broughton Architects/Creative Commons; 21 bottom left, Red Fox studio/Shutterstock; 22 top, frank60/Shutterstock; 22 middle, F.Neidl/Shutterstock; 22 bottom, DedeDian/Shutterstock; 23 top right, Alain Mazaud/Creative Commons; 23 top, ymgerman/Shutterstock; 23 middle, Alexey Seafarer/Shutterstock; 23 bottom left, xolmgard/Shutterstock; 24 top, Ivan Hoermann/Shutte·stock; 24 bottom, Anton_Ivanov/Shutterstock; 24 bottom left, Anders Beer Wilse/Public Domain; 24 bottom right, Herbert Ponting/Public Domain; 25 top, Lawrence Oates/Public Domain; 24 middle, Felicity Aston/Creative Commons; 25 bottom, NASA/Cindy Evans/Public Domain; 24 Carobassignana/Creative Commons; 24 left, Real Sports Photos/Shutterstock; 25 top, Daniel Leussler/Creative Commons; 25 bottom, Anton Rodionov/Shutterstock; 25 bottom left, Phil West/Shutterstock; 25 bottom middel, Pixel-Shot/Shutterstock; 26 top, ANDRE DIB/Shutterstock; 26 bottom left, Ion Mes/Shutterstock; 26 top right, Gts/Shutterstock; 28-29, Austen Photography

Bearport Publishing Company Product Development Team

President: Jen Jenson; Director of Product Development: Spencer Brinker; Managing Editor: Allison Juda; Associate Editor: Naomi Reich; Associate Editor: Tiana Tran; Art Director: Colin O'Dea; Designer: Elena Klinkner; Designer: Kayla Eggert; Product Development Assistant: Owen Hamlin

Produced for Bearport Publishing by BlueAppleWorks Inc.
Managing Editor for BlueAppleWorks: Melissa McClellan
Art Director: T.J. Choleva
Photo Research: Jane Reid

STATEMENT ON USAGE OF GENERATIVE ARTIFICIAL INTELLIGENCE
Bearport Publishing remains committed to publishing high-quality nonfiction books. Therefore, we restrict the use of generative AI to ensure accuracy of all text and visual components pertaining to a book's subject. See BearportPublishing.com for details.

Library of Congress Cataloging-in-Publication Data

Names: Finan, Catherine C., 1972- author.
Title: Antarctica / by Catherine C. Finan.
Description: Minneapolis, Minnesota : Bearport Publishing Company, [2024] | Series: X-treme facts. Continents | Includes bibliographical references and index.
Identifiers: LCCN 2023030970 (print) | LCCN 2023030971 (ebook) | ISBN 9798889164357 (hardcover) | ISBN 9798889164432 (paperback) | ISBN 9798889164500 (ebook)
Subjects: LCSH: Antarctica--Juvenile literature. | Antarctica--Discovery and exploration.
Classification: LCC G863 .F56 2024 (print) | LCC G863 (ebook) | DDC 919.89--dc23/eng/20230818
LC record available at https://lccn.loc.gov/2023030970
LC ebook record available at https://lccn.loc.gov/2023030971

Copyright © 2024 Bearport Publishing Company. All rights reserved. No part of this publication may be reproduced in whole or in part, stored in any retrieval system, or transmitted in any form or by any means, electronic, mechanical, photocopying, recording, or otherwise, without written permission from the publisher.

For more information, write to Bearport Publishing, 5357 Penn Avenue South, Minneapolis, MN 55419.

Contents

The Most Extreme Continent 4

A Frozen Desert 6

Coldest of the Cold 8

Volcanoes in a Land of Ice 10

Ghost Mountains, Buried Lakes 12

A Lake of Blood? 14

Diamonds in the Air 16

Wait, What Time Is It? 18

Treaty for an Empty Landscape 20

Awesome Antarctic Animals 22

Antarctic Adventures 24

Meet Me in Antarctica! 26

Snow Time 28

Glossary 30

Read More 31

Learn More Online 31

Index 32

About the Author 32

The Most Extreme Continent

Imagine a place so cold, you'd get **frostbite** in minutes if you weren't wearing the proper clothing outside. Imagine somewhere so windy, gusts reaching 200 miles per hour (320 kph) blow across the frozen landscape. Imagine being somewhere so **desolate**, you may be the only living being for miles. You've just pictured Antarctica—the most extreme place on Earth. It's time to bundle up and explore Earth's coldest, windiest, and driest **continent** . . . if you dare!

Antarctica means opposite of the Arctic. The Arctic is Earth's northernmost region. Antarctica is the southernmost part of the planet.

TURN THE GLOBE UPSIDE DOWN TO SPOT THIS CONTINENT!

Antarctica is Earth's fifth-largest continent.

The thickest part of Antarctica's ice sheet is about 3 miles (5 km). That's almost half the height of Mt. Everest!

If Antarctica's ice sheet melted, Earth's sea levels would rise by 200 feet (60 m). Cities along coasts would be underwater.

A Frozen Desert

You might think a place as cold and icy as Antarctica is the exact opposite of a desert. Wrong! We usually think of deserts as having superhot temperatures, blowing sand, and cacti. But really, a desert is any **habitat** that gets very little **precipitation**. It has nothing to do with the temperature or landscape. Antarctica is considered a polar desert. The continent gets less precipitation than Africa's Sahara Desert.

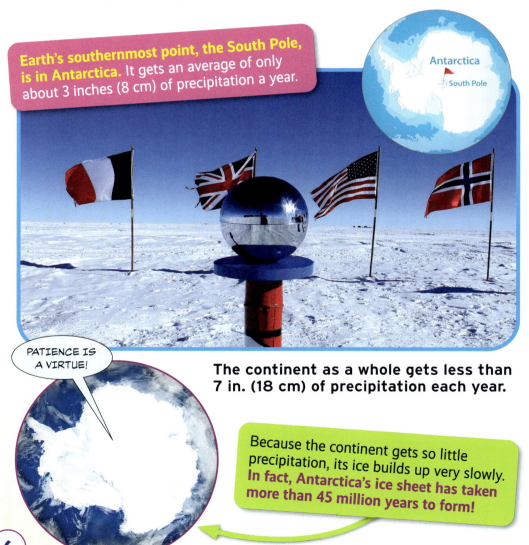

Earth's southernmost point, the South Pole, is in Antarctica. It gets an average of only about 3 inches (8 cm) of precipitation a year.

PATIENCE IS A VIRTUE!

The continent as a whole gets less than 7 in. (18 cm) of precipitation each year.

Because the continent gets so little precipitation, its ice builds up very slowly. In fact, Antarctica's ice sheet has taken more than 45 million years to form!

Only about 2 percent of Antarctica is always free of ice and snow. These areas are called the McMurdo Dry Valleys. They have some of Earth's harshest desert conditions.

Scientists believe these valleys haven't gotten any rain or snow in about two million years!

Scientists think conditions in these dry valleys are similar to those on the surface of Mars.

Coldest of the Cold

So just how cold does it get in Antarctica? Very, very cold! On July 21, 1983, scientists at Vostok Station in Antarctica measured the temperature at an incredibly cold -128 degrees Fahrenheit (-89 degrees Celsius). Surely that's as cold as Earth can get, right? Nope! In 2010, scientists used **satellite** data to record an even colder temperature of -144°F (-98°C) in the middle of the Antarctic ice sheet. That's like being on a different planet!

At -144°F (-98°C), just a few breaths of air would make your lungs bleed. Death would soon follow.

Mars has an average temperature of -81°F (-63°C). That's tropical compared to Antarctica at its coldest.

Scientists think Earth can't get any colder than the record low set on Antarctica.

Many millions of years ago, Antarctica was much warmer. Fossils show it was also covered in forests.

Despite Antarctica's extreme cold, some scientists do research there year-round. Now that's brave!

The continent isn't always cold. In 2020, the Antarctic **Peninsula** warmed up to about 65°F (18°C).

Volcanoes in a Land of Ice

In this frozen land, you might not expect to see a volcano. But Antarctica is full of surprises. The continent is home to many volcanoes—two of which are active. Mt. Erebus is the southernmost volcano on Earth. The other active volcano is in Antarctica's South Shetland Islands. This sunken volcano forms Deception Island. The volcano is under water and ice, so from the surface, you'd never know it was still active.

Mt. Erebus is one of Earth's few active volcanoes with a permanent lava lake in its crater.

Mt. Erebus's lava lake is 1,700°F (930°C). That's some hot stuff in a cold place!

In 1908, scientist Edgeworth David led the first climb of Mt. Erebus. The difficult 12,500-ft (3,800-m) trip took five days.

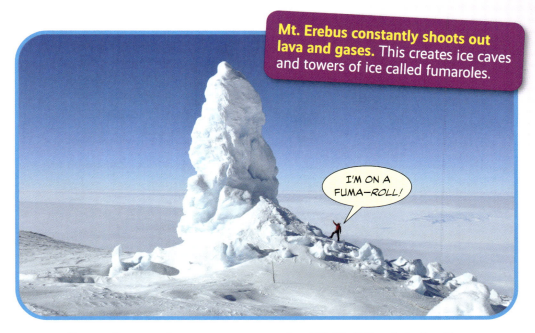

Some fumaroles can grow up to 60 ft (18 m) tall—the same height as four giraffes standing on top of each other.

About 15,000 tourists visit Deception Island each year. Would you make the trip?

Ghost Mountains, Buried Lakes

While Mt. Erebus towers above Antarctica's landscape, some of the continent's secrets are more hidden. The Gamburtsev Mountains stretch out for more than 750 miles (1,200 km) underneath Antarctica's thick ice! The continent is also home to about 600 lakes beneath the ice. These lakes are warmed by Earth's core, so they never freeze despite being on a chilly continent.

Antarctica's buried Lake Mercer is full of **bacteria**. Scientists think it **might have hidden forms of life.**

WOW! THAT IS ONE GIANT ICICLE!

Scientist had to drill through about 3,570 ft (1,090 m) of ice to get samples of Lake Mercer's water.

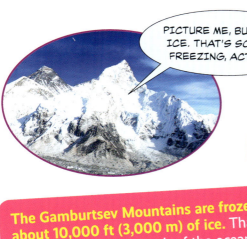

"PICTURE ME, BURIED IN ICE. THAT'S SO COOL! FREEZING, ACTUALLY."

The buried Gamburtsev Mountains reach impressive heights. **Their tallest peaks are around 11,000 ft (3,000 m) high—about one-third the height of Mt. Everest.**

The Gamburtsev Mountains are frozen in about 10,000 ft (3,000 m) of ice. That's almost the average depth of the ocean.

"TRUST ME, THEY'RE DOWN THERE...."

"WHAT MOUNTAINS? I DON'T SEE ANY MOUNTAINS!"

No one has ever seen the underground mountains with their own eyes.

"I SEE YOU!"

How do we know the Gamburtsev Mountains are there? **Special instruments show scientists pictures of what's below the thick ice.**

13

A Lake of Blood?

Could this cold continent be hiding a darker, bloody secret, too? It may sound like something out of a horror movie, but in 1911, a strange sight on a **glacier** in eastern Antarctica stopped scientists in their tracks. Water flowing from inside Taylor Glacier was staining the ice a bright, bloody red. For more than 100 years, no one could find the cause. But in 2017, scientists finally discovered the secret of this Antarctic mystery! Thankfully, no Antarctic creatures were harmed in the making of the red lake.

The creepy coloring of the glacier inspired the horrific nickname **Blood Falls!**

WHEN I SAID WE COULD USE A BIT OF COLOR, I DIDN'T MEAN BLOOD!

Taylor Glacier was named after **geologist** Thomas Griffith Taylor, who saw the glacier during an **expedition** in the early 1900s.

At first, scientists thought Taylor Glacier's red color was caused by a kind of **algae**. But that's not right.

Water flowing from Taylor Glacier comes from an underground lake containing salt and iron.

THAT GLACIER MUST BE VERY OLD.

YEAH, IT'S ALL RUSTY!

When water from inside the glacier meets air, the oxygen causes the iron to rust. This turns the water blood-red. *Eeeek!*

Rare bacteria on the glacier survive with almost no oxygen. **Scientists study them to understand how life might exist on other planets.**

15

Diamonds in the Air

Seeing what looks like a bloody waterfall during an Antarctic visit would be shocking. But what if you thought you saw diamonds sparkling in the air around you? Depending on weather conditions, moisture in the Antarctic air freezes into tiny ice crystals. This amazing visual display is called diamond dust because it looks like tiny diamonds glittering all around.

Diamond dust happens when there are clear skies. Sunshine lights up the ice crystals in the air, making them sparkle.

Antarctica's diamond dust is usually seen when temperatures drop below 14°F (-10°C).

IT MIGHT BE FREEZING, BUT IT'S SPECTACULAR!

16

Antarctica's diamond dust can create another incredible sight—sun dogs. These are bright spots that appear in the sky on either side of the sun.

An average ice crystal is about as wide as a human hair.

The human eye can barely see a single ice crystal. We can see diamond dust because there are so many crystals in the air.

Wait, What Time Is It?

You'll see diamond dust sparkling best in the Antarctic sunshine . . . but only during the summer when the sun actually shines. In winter, there are months of constant darkness. No matter which season, time itself is measured a bit differently at the very bottom of the world. Antarctica has no official time zones. For the researchers living there, this can cause a bit of confusion.

Antarctica has only two seasons—winter and summer. Each lasts for six months.

During Antarctica's winter, the continent is in darkness. Summer has six months of daylight.

X MARKS THE SPOT!

Earth's lines of **longitude** divide the planet into its different time zones. These lines all come together and meet at the South Pole.

Sometimes, scientists follow the time zone of the country closest to their station. The United States' Palmer Station follows the time zone of Chile.

McMurdo Station is Antarctica's largest research center. It's run by the United States, but it follows New Zealand time since that's the closest country.

Treaty for an Empty Landscape

Whether winter or summer, Antarctica is a difficult place to reach. In fact, humans had probably never laid eyes on it until 1820. When Antarctica was discovered, there was nobody living there full-time. So, many countries quickly claimed ownership. That led to some tensions. Finally, almost 140 years later, several countries signed a treaty to share Antarctica as a place for research. That agreement continues today.

On January 27, 1820, explorers Fabian Gottlieb von Bellingshausen and Mikhail Lazarev **were the first Europeans to officially discover mainland Antarctica.**

WITHOUT A DOUBT, SIR!

DO YOU THINK WE'LL GO DOWN IN HISTORY FOR FINDING THIS CHUNK OF ICE?

It took another 20 years before Antarctica was considered a continent rather than just a group of islands.

It's possible that people from islands in the Pacific Ocean discovered Antarctica more than 1,000 years earlier, but it's hard to find evidence of this history.

A group of 12 countries signed the Antarctic Treaty on December 1, 1959. This agreement said they would share the land peacefully.

So far, about 50 countries have signed the treaty. They have regular meetings to decide how research should be handled on the continent.

The different countries work together *to make sure the Antarctic Treaty is being upheld.*

Today, there are more than 80 research stations on Antarctica.

PEACE, LOVE, AND RESEARCH!

Awesome Antarctic Animals

Some researchers in Antarctica study the continent's awesome animal life. Conditions are so harsh that many animals can't live there at all. The animals that do call the place home are incredibly tough. They often have amazing **adaptations** to live in this extreme climate—such as fish with **antifreeze** in their blood to keep from becoming ice in the cold Antarctic waters. Let's go on an Antarctic animal adventure to learn more.

Does this continent have the right name? **Not a single ant lives in *Ant*-arctica!**

HONESTLY, CAN YOU BLAME US?

THAT'S RIGHT! WE LIKE IT HOT!

The most common land animal in Antarctica is the **nematode worm**.

Hate snakes? Move to Antarctica! It's the only continent without them—or any other reptiles.

During the summer, Antarctica is home to eight **species** of penguins!

TRY TO KEEP UP, SLACKERS!

Antarctica's Gentoo penguins are the fastest penguins in the world, clocking in at 22 miles per hour (35 kph).

Polar bears are sometimes thought of as an Antarctic animal. But they only live in the Arctic—on the opposite end of Earth.

IS THAT WHY I NEVER GET MY MAIL?

Male emperor penguins are the only warm-blooded animals that don't leave before winter arrives. They keep their eggs warm while female emperor penguins spend months at sea feeding.

YOU GOTTA DO WHAT YOU GOTTA DO!

Antarctic Adventures

Even with all we know about Antarctica, there is still so much left to discover. Most of the continent has never been seen. Over the past 200 years, explorers have braved extreme conditions to learn more about this ice-covered land. From a race to the South Pole in the early 1900s to modern research about this icy world, some attempts were successful, and others failed—badly.

Each year, Antarctica has just one full sunrise (in September) and one full sunset (in March). Explorers need to plan their visits wisely!

On December 14, 1911, Norway's Roald Amundsen was the first person to reach the South Pole. He beat England's Robert Falcon Scott by a month.

WHAT TOOK YOU SO LONG, SCOTT?

I TOOK A WRONG TURN. ALL THIS ICE LOOKS THE SAME!

Amundsen and his team all returned to the base camp safely. Sadly, Scott and his team died during their return trip.

Meet Me in Antarctica!

Studying Antarctica's landscape, climate, and life-forms helps researchers better understand this extreme and fascinating place. Through this work, we're learning more about how humans might survive in such challenging conditions. Maybe one day we'll use this knowledge to live on the moon or even Mars! So, whether visiting on vacation or as a researcher, there is still so much left to discover on this supercool continent.

If you stood at the South Pole, every direction you looked would be north!

HEY, DUDE! WE'RE SUPPOSED TO RUN NORTH!

I *AM* RUNNING NORTH!

Are you crazy enough to try a marathon on Antarctica? Every year, people shell out more than $20,000 for the experience!

Antarctica has its own highway. This unpaved road is about 1,000 miles (1,600 km) long and allows people to bring supplies to the South Pole.

In 2013, **the band Metallica played a concert on the frozen continent.** Now that's cool!

There have been researchers at the Amundsen-Scott South Pole Station since 1956. During summer, about 150 people call it home.

At the South Pole, you'll see flags from all the countries that signed the Antarctic Treaty.

Each year, about 70,000 postcards are mailed from Antarctica's Penguin Post Office—a remote post office surrounded by penguins.

Snow Time

Activity

Antarctica doesn't get much snow, and any that does fall rarely melts because of the freezing temperatures. Over time, this snow builds up, forming the thick ice sheets that cover the continent. Make your own snow and see if you can turn it into an icy layer.

What You Will Need

- Baking soda
- A measuring cup
- A large bowl
- A tablespoon
- Water
- A fork
- A plastic tray
- Optional: penguin figurines

Though it gets little snow every year, most of the snow that does fall doesn't melt.

The snow builds up over many years to make the large ice sheets.

Step One

Pour 3 cups of baking soda into a bowl.

Step Two

Add 1 tablespoon of water. Use a fork to stir the ingredients together.

Step Three

Add water a tablespoon at a time, mixing thoroughly between, until you have a snow-like consistency. You should be able to make a mini snowball.

Step Four

Place the fake snow in your tray. Make mounds of fake snow and press it down to create the Antarctic ice sheets. You can add penguin figurines to your landscape if you'd like.

adaptations changes to animals or plants that help them survive in their environment

algae plantlike living things that are found in water and can make their own food

antifreeze a substance that lowers the freezing point of a liquid

bacteria tiny living things that can be seen only under a microscope

continent one of the world's seven large land masses

desolate with very few of living things

expedition a long trip taken for a specific reason, such as exploring

frostbite the freezing of skin due to exposure to extreme cold

geologist a scientist who studies Earth's rocks and soil

glacier a large mass of ice formed from firmly packed snow

habitat a place in nature where an animal lives

longitude distance measured on Earth's surface east or west of an imaginary line on the globe that goes from the North Pole to the South Pole

meteorites pieces of rock from outer space that have landed on Earth

peninsula land surrounded by water on three sides

precipitation water that falls to the ground in the form of rain, snow, sleet, or hail

satellite a spacecraft that circles the planet to gather information and send it back to Earth

species groups that living things are divided into according to similar characteristics

Read More

Aspen-Baxter, Linda. *Antarctica (Exploring Continents).* New York: Lightbox Learning Inc., 2023.

Dickmann, Nancy. *Death at the South Pole! Antarctica, 1911-1912 (Doomed History).* Minneapolis: Bearport Publishing Company, 2023.

Morey, Allan. *Exploring Antarctica (Dangerous Journeys).* Minneapolis: Bellwether Media, Inc., 2023.

Learn More Online

1. Go to **www.factsurfer.com** or scan the QR code below.

2. Enter "**X-treme Antarctica**" into the search box.

3. Click on the cover of this book to see a list of websites.

Index

Amundsen, Roald 24–25
Amundsen-Scott South Pole Station 27
Antarctic Peninsula 9
Antarctic Treaty 20–21, 27
Aston, Felicity 25
Blood Falls 14, 16
Deception Island 10–11
desert 6–7
diamond dust 16–18
dry valleys 7
Gamburtsev Mountains 12–13
ice sheet 5–6, 8, 28–29

McMurdo Research Station 19
meteorites 25
Mt. Erebus 10–12
penguins 9, 23, 27
research 9, 11, 18–22, 24, 26–27
Scott, Robert Falcon 24–25
South Pole 6, 18, 24–27
Taylor Glacier 14–15
time zones 18–19
volcanoes 10
Vostok Station 8
wind 4

About the Author

Catherine C. Finan is a writer living in northeastern Pennsylvania. So far, she's been to five of Earth's seven continents. Antarctica and Australia are next on her list of places to visit!